The Pint Sized Pirate

By

D. M. Larson

Copyright (c) 2003, 2014 For permission to perform this
All Rights Reserved   play, contact
                        doug@freedrama.net

PEGGY THE PINT SIZED PIRATE (30 MINUTE FEMALE VERSION)

(14 characters plus optional extras)

CAST OF CHARACTERS

PEGGY - a small pirate who sets out to rescue the pirates from a sea monster SCUMMY - young pirate who says mean things to PEGGY BOB - the Brave can be either gender (Bob can be short for Roberta). One of the mean pirates who pick on PEGGY. SUE - the Smelly can be changed to Sam. Another mean pirate.

CAPTAIN SLUDGE - Pirate Captain who wants to plunder and pillage Arizona

CAPTAIN SOGGY - Pirate Captain who secretly wants to open a sea side resort

GRUNT - wise old pirate who speaks mysteriously

MERMAID - helps PEGGY find the sea monster

WILLY the whale - someone who knows the way to the sea monster

BARNEY the barnacle - attached to the whale and mocks the whale constantly

PEARL the oyster - a game show host

VOICE of game show announcer

SEA MONSTER - a baby sea monster who helps his mama capture the pirates

MAMA MONSTER - a sea monster mother that is angry at the pirates for littering in her ocean

EXTRAS - Other PIRATES and OYSTERS

SCENES

Scene 1 - A pirate's cove for games and grub

Scene 2 - On the high seas

Scene 3 - An island where the Sea Monster lurks

SCENE 1

(CONTINUED)

CONTINUED: 2.

(PEGGY is a very small pirate girl who is anxious to be a big pirate. PEGGY enters pirate's cove and sees Pirates playing various games and enjoying grub. Everyone is much bigger than she is and she looks out of place)

          PEGGY
     (To audience)
Hi, I'm Peggy. Peggy the... Well, I don't have a true pirate name yet.

          SCUMMY
     (To PEGGY)
Sure you do. It's Peggy the Pint Sized Pirate.

(Other pirates laugh and then go back to their games)

          PEGGY
Yes, that's what they call me. Peggy the Pint Sized Pirate. But I'm tired of it. I won't stand for it anymore.

          SCUMMY
Won't stand for it? I thought you were sitting down.

          PEGGY
I'm so tired of short jokes. Anyway... Today is my big day. I finally was going to be a pirate. I've dreamed about this day since I was little.
     (SCUMMY looks at her)
Well, I'm still little... and I'm still dreaming. But finally the day has come. I'm going to do it. I'm going to be a pirate.

(BOB and SUE come and inspect PEGGY)

          BOB
No way. Pirates have to be big.

          SUE
And they have to be strong.

(SUE holds out her hand to arm wrestle PEGGY)

          SCUMMY
You scared that Sue will hurt you Peggy.

(CONTINUED)

CONTINUED: 3.

> PEGGY
> I know I'm not as strong as you but I know I'll be a good pirate. I'm a hard worker.

> BOB
> Hard worker? Some of the best pirates are lazy.

> PEGGY
> And I'm sharp as a tack.

> SUE
> The only sharp thing a pirate needs is her sword.

(Pokes at PEGGY with her sword)

> PEGGY
> So if I'm not a big, dumb, lazy killer than I can't be a pirate?

(BOB Looks at SUE, then at PEGGY)

> BOB
> Pretty much.

(SUE and BOB go back to what they were doing)

> PEGGY
> There must be someone who would like a hard working thinker like me.

(SCUMMY laughs at her and then points to CAPTAINS who enter)

> SCUMMY
> Line em up!

(Pirates line up. PEGGY gets stuck behind the other pirates and hops around trying to see. She slips in between two of them)

> CAPTAIN SOGGY
> We need two crews for a treasure run to Tucson.

> PEGGY
> Tucson?

(PEGGY gets pushed back and hops around behind)

(CONTINUED)

CONTINUED: 4.

                    CAPTAIN SLUDGE
          I get first pick. I'll take Bob the
          Brave.

(BOB happily lines up behind SLUDGE)

                    CAPTAIN SOGGY
          I'll take Sue the Smelly.

(Everyone steps back so SUE can move over by SOGGY who
notices her odor. SLUDGE and SOGGY continue picking pirates
during the following:)

                    PEGGY
          I was so excited. This was the
          first time I tried out for a pirate
          crew. Captain Sludge had the
          fastest pirate around. Everyone was
          anxious to be with Sludge when the
          sea speed record of 1812 was
          broken. And then Captain Soggy was
          great too. Soggy had the only
          pirate ship that would go
          underwater. Really! But after more
          and more pirates were picked, I got
          worried because no one was picking
          me.

                    CAPTAIN SLUDGE
          And I'll take Scummy the Sweet.

(SCUMMY sticks tongue out at PEGGY and lines up with others)

                    CAPTAIN SOGGY
          That's it then.

(Pirates all start to talk and go with CAPTAINS)

                    PEGGY
          Wait! What about me?!

(Everyone stops and stares at PEGGY. Then they laugh)

                    SCUMMY
          No way, shrimp.

(CAPTAIN SOGGY pats PEGGY on the head)

                    CAPTAIN SOGGY
          Maybe when you're bigger.

                                                        (CONTINUED)

CONTINUED:

                    SCUMMY
Right, that will happen.

                  CAPTAIN SLUDGE
Better stay here and let the big brave pirates go. We don't want you to get hurt.

                  CAPTAIN SOGGY
We can't handle screaming little girls on ships with sea monster afoot.

(Pirates leave and PEGGY sits by herself all upset)

                    PEGGY
Now I'll never be a pirate.

(PEGGY cries. Old GRUNT enters)

                    GRUNT
What's this boo-hooing I hear?

                    PEGGY
No one wants me to be a pirate. They think I'm too little.

                    GRUNT
Do they now?

                    PEGGY
Everyone laughed at me and said I'd be scared. I'm not scared of anything. And I wouldn't cry.
    (Wipes away tears)
I'm not afraid of any sea monsters.
    (Cries again)
Who am I kidding? I am too little.

                    GRUNT
You're not little at all you know.

                    PEGGY
What? Can't you see me? I'm tiny.

                    GRUNT
There's something I can see that's bigger than any pirate I know. Something that you'll have to see on your own.

(CONTINUED)

CONTINUED:

>   PEGGY
>   I don't get it. What do you mean?
>
>   GRUNT
>   Give it time, Peggy and you'll see.
>
>   PEGGY
>   (Throwing a fit)
>   But I wanna be big now!!!!!

(PEGGY Jumps around and screams. GRUNT waits for PEGGY to stop)

>   GRUNT
>   Feel better?

(Peggy sighs and is calm now)

>   PEGGY
>   Actually, yes. Thank you.
>
>   GRUNT
>   Very soon you'll get your chance to
>   see what you have that is greater
>   than most.
>
>   PEGGY
>   Well, I'm not moving from this spot
>   until I find out.
>
>   GRUNT
>   Stubborn aren't we?
>
>   PEGGY
>   Peggy the Stubborn. Naw, doesn't
>   sound right.
>
>   GRUNT
>   Patience Peggy. Your moment will
>   come.

(GRUNT leaves)

>   PEGGY
>   Old people saw the weirdest things.
>   Me being big? Now? But how? Little
>   did I know that out at sea,
>   something was about to happen that
>   would change my life forever.

(CONTINUED)

CONTINUED: 7.

(A make shift sea and pirate ship is pushed in at one side of the stage by PIRATES and another make shift sea and ship is pushed in on the opposite side. CAPTAIN SLUDGE, BOB and other PIRATES are in one boat. CAPTAIN SOGGY and SUE and other PIRATES are in the other)

                CAPTAIN SOGGY
Set sail for Tucson!

                SUE
Captain. I see something.

(SEA MONSTER pops up from sea and does a Jaws impression)

                SEA MONSTER
Da-dum.

                SUE
Did you see it?

                CAPTAIN SOGGY
No.

                SEA MONSTER
Da-dum.

                SUE
There!

                CAPTAIN SOGGY
Whale ho!

                SEA MONSTER
Da-dum.

                SUE
That's no whale.

                CAPTAIN SOGGY
It's a...

                SUE AND SOGGY
SEA MONSTER!

                SEA MONSTER
Da-da, da-da, da-da.

(SEA MONSTER attacks ship)

                CAPTAIN SOGGY
Everyone pirate for himself!

(CAPTAIN SOGGY runs away screaming)

(CONTINUED)

CONTINUED: 8.

> SUE
> Help! It's got me.

(SEA MONSTER drags off SUE and other PIRATES. Sinks ship #1. CAPTAIN SLUDGE watches all this with his spy glass)

> CAPTAIN SLUDGE
> Now wasn't that something.

> BOB
> What'd you see?

> CAPTAIN SLUDGE
> Looked like Captain Soggy's ship was sunk by a sea monster.

> BOB
> Sea monster? Are you mad?

> SEA MONSTER
> (Appears)
> Did somebody say Sea Monster?

> BOB
> There it is!

(SEA MONSTER disappears)

> CAPTAIN SLUDGE
> Where?

> BOB
> It's gone.

> CAPTAIN SLUDGE
> Likely story. I think you're seeing things.

(SEA MONSTER pops up so CAPTAIN can't see)

> SEA MONSTER
> Yoo-hoo.

> BOB
> There it is again!

(CAPTAIN SLUDGE turns. SEA MONSTER disappears)

> CAPTAIN SLUDGE
> Where?

(CONTINUED)

CONTINUED: 9.

>   BOB
> Right there. I swear.
>
>   CAPTAIN SLUDGE
> That's it. One more outburst out of
> you and you'll walk the plank.
>
>   SEA MONSTER
> Yoo-hoo.

(SEA MONSTER waves at BOB who points frantically but CAPTAIN SLUDGE is turned away. SEA MONSTER grabs BOB and other PIRATES)

>   BOB
> Mommy.

(CAPTAIN SLUDGE is left alone)

>   CAPTAIN SLUDGE
> It's so quiet. It's like I'm
> totally alone.
>   (Looks)
> Where is everybody? (Looks down)
> Why is my ship filling with water?
>
>   SEA MONSTER
>   (Appears)
> I believe you're sinking.
>
>   CAPTAIN SLUDGE
> You think so?
>
>   SEA MONSTER
> Most definitely.
>
>   CAPTAIN SLUDGE
> Are you sure?
>
>   SEA MONSTER
> Quite. Because I put the hole in it
> myself.
>
>   CAPTAIN SLUDGE
> Oh dear. You're not...
>
>   SEA MONSTER
> I am.
>
>   CAPTAIN SLUDGE
> Oh dear. I better...

(CONTINUED)

CONTINUED: 10.

                    SEA MONSTER
        Run!

(CAPTAIN SLUDGE screams and runs and SEA MONSTER sinks ship. Scene goes back to PEGGY at Pirate's Cove)

                    SCUMMY
          (Runs in)
        Ahh! The horror! The horror!

                    PEGGY
        What is it, Scummy?

                    SCUMMY
        Both ships are gone. Destroyed.

                    PEGGY
        But how?

                    SCUMMY
        The sea monster!

                    PEGGY
        Really? And the pirates couldn't
        stop them.

                    SCUMMY
        They tried but the monster is too
        powerful. Both ships are gone
        forever.

                    PEGGY
        How did you survive?

                    SCUMMY
        I hid in a barrel when I saw the
        monster coming.

                    PEGGY
        You hid? That's not very piratey.

                    SCUMMY
        Please don't tell.

(SCUMMY runs and hides. CAPTAIN SLUDGE enters with CAPTAIN SOGGY)

                  CAPTAIN SLUDGE
        I can't believe our ships are gone.

                  CAPTAIN SOGGY
        And the entire crew was captured.

                                                (CONTINUED)

CONTINUED:

                PEGGY
What are you going to do?

                CAPTAIN SLUDGE
What can we do?

                CAPTAIN SOGGY
Maybe I'll open up a little sea side resort.

                PEGGY
You can't give up. What about your crew? You must save them.

                CAPTAIN SLUDGE
Sorry, but I'm not going out there again. Not with that monster out there.

                CAPTAIN SOGGY
And I could serve soda pop and soup with little tiny umbrellas in them.

                PEGGY
So you're both a couple of chickens.

(Both CAPTAINS stop and stare at her)

                CAPTAIN SLUDGE
What did you say?

                PEGGY
Chickens.
    (Acts like a chicken)
Brock, brock, brock.

                CAPTAIN SOGGY
I could put chicken between two slices of bread. Someone showed me that on the Sandwich Islands.

(CAPTAIN SOGGY exits)

                CAPTAIN SLUDGE
Fine. You think you're so brave. Then you be captain and take care of that sea monster yourself.
    (Sticks huge captain hat on
    PEGGY and it covers her head)
Best of luck to you, Captain.

(CAPTAIN SLUDGE laughs and exits. PEGGY pulls off the hat)

(CONTINUED)

CONTINUED: 12.

PEGGY
Captain? Was he serious? Even if he wasn't, it doesn't matter. Someone has to save those pirates. (Grabs SCUMMY out of hiding) Come on, Scummy. We're going to save some pirates.

SCENE 2

(PEGGY and SCUMMY appear in a small boat [they can carry out a cutout of a boat that they carry on and stand behind].)

PEGGY
So I set sail trying to find our missing pirate friends. I knew that if I could save them, then I would prove that I was worthy of being a pirate.

SCUMMY
And I knew if I went along, the captains couldn't find me and string me up for running away.

PEGGY
But they ran away too. How can they get mad at you?

SCUMMY
Good point. Let's go back and tell them that.

PEGGY
No, we've already come this far. We're not going back.

SCUMMY
But I'm...

PEGGY
You're what?

SCUMMY
I'm scared, okay? Happy now.

PEGGY
It's okay to be scared.

SCUMMY
No, it's not. Pirates don't get scared.

(CONTINUED)

CONTINUED: 13.

> PEGGY
> I'll bet they do. They just don't tell anyone. But it's okay to get scared.

> SCUMMY
> Are you scared?

> PEGGY
> For some reason, no. I'm not sure why. You think I would be but I'm so set on finding those lost pirates that I haven't thought about being scared.

> SCUMMY
> Wow, Peggy. You're really something.

> PEGGY
> Hey, did you just say something nice to me?

> SCUMMY
> (Embarrassed)
> No.

> PEGGY
> Yes, you did.

> SCUMMY
> Can we stop talking now?

(Piles of broken ships are pushed in on opposite side of stage)

> PEGGY
> Look. Over there.

> SCUMMY
> What is it?

(MERMAID appears in front of them)

> MERMAID
> It's a pirate ship graveyard.

> PEGGY
> What a mess.

> SCUMMY
> Who are you?

(CONTINUED)

CONTINUED: 14.

                MERMAID
I'm Oceanna.

                PEGGY
A mermaid.

                MERMAID
This is my home. But it's ruined.

                PEGGY
What happened?

                MERMAID
The pirates came here looking for treasure. The sea monster got mad and destroyed their ships.

                PEGGY
The sea monster? Can you help me find it?

                MERMAID
Why would you want to do that? Can't you see what happened to the last pirates who tried?

                PEGGY
I want to free the pirates that it captured.

                MERMAID
You are very brave little pirate.

                SCUMMY
No, she's just crazy.

                MERMAID
It's not safe. Please turn back before you meet the same fate as the others.

                SCUMMY
Good idea. Let's go home.

                PEGGY
I can't. I have sworn an oath to help them. Can't you show us the way?

                MERMAID
I don't know the way.... but I think I know someone who does. I'll see if they'll talk to you.

(CONTINUED)

CONTINUED: 15.

                    PEGGY
Thank you.

(MERMAID goes)

                    SCUMMY
I can't believe you're asking for help.

                    PEGGY
What's wrong with that?

                    SCUMMY
Pirates don't ask for help. We do everything by instinct.

                    PEGGY
No wonder you're always getting lost.

(WILLY is a whale [played by a bigger actor] and has BARNEY the barnacle [played by a smaller actor] attached to him)

                    WILLY
The mermaid said were looking for some directions.

                    BARNEY
Directions? You'd get lost in a bathtub.

                    WILLY
Quiet you.

                    BARNEY
       (Mocking) Quiet you.

                    WILLY
Will you get off of me?

                    BARNEY
Will you get off of me?

                    SCUMMY
What is wrong with you guys?

                    WILLY
Barney here is a barnacle. Us whales get stuck with them sometimes.

(CONTINUED)

CONTINUED: 16.

                SCUMMY
Can't you get rid of him?

                WILLY
I've been trying.

                BARNEY
I've been trying... but you're stuck with me baby.

                PEGGY
Excuse me. I do hate to bother you, but do you know the way to the Sea Monster's lair?

                WILLY AND BARNEY
The Sea Monster!

                WILLY
You don't want to go there.

                BARNEY
The Sea Monster hates pirates.

                SCUMMY
So we'd go home then.

                PEGGY
No, we're going.

                WILLY
Looks like you have a barnacle too.

(WILLY and BARNEY laugh)

                SCUMMY
I'm not a barnacle. She's the barnacle. I'm stuck with her.

                WILLY
Why do you want to find the Sea Monster anyway?

                PEGGY
We have to save the other pirates.

                WILLY
But I don't like pirates. Why should I help you?

                BARNEY
Cause I do.
         (Points)
              (MORE)

(CONTINUED)

CONTINUED: 17.

       BARNEY (cont'd)
  It's that way.

       WILLY
  Don't tell them that.

       BARNEY
  Don't tell them that.

(WILLY starts to drag off BARNEY)

       PEGGY
  Thanks.

       BARNEY
  Any time.

(BARNEY is dragged off by WILLY)

       SCUMMY
  Weirdoes.

       PEGGY
  Let's go then.

       SCUMMY
  Do we have to? I got you this far.
  But this is where I turned back
  before and I plan to again.

       PEGGY
  Come on, Scummy. Don't you want to
  be a hero.

       SCUMMY
  A hero?

       PEGGY
  If you rescue the pirates, you'll
  probably get a whole treasure chest
  of gold.

       SCUMMY
    (Brightens)
  Gold?

       PEGGY
  I bet they'll make you captain.

       SCUMMY
    (Excited)
  Captain? (Smiles) Let's go!

(CONTINUED)

CONTINUED: 18.

      PEGGY
  Let's.

(PEGGY and SCUMMY make a motion like they are swimming and OYSTERS appear ahead of them. PEARL is the head OYSTER and is like a game show host. The other OYSTERS are like a studio audience. If extras are not available, someone could hold up signs to the audience and the audience could do the OYSTER lines)

      PEARL
  Thank you for tuning in to the...

     PEARL AND OYSTERS
  WHEEL! OF! MISFORTUNE!

(Wheel of Misfortune is rolled out)

      PEARL
  I'm your host Pearl Jam.
    (OYSTERS cheer)
  And I see we have a couple of new contestants. (Goes to PEGGY and SCUMMY) Please tell us your names and a little bit about yourselves.

      PEGGY
  Hi, I'm Peggy.

      OYSTERS
  Hi, Peggy.

      PEGGY
  And I'm looking for some pirates who were kidnapped by a sea monster.

      OYSTERS
  Aaah!

      PEARL
  How exciting!
    (To SCUMMY)
  And you are?

      SCUMMY
  None of your business.

      OYSTERS
  Oooh!

        (CONTINUED)

CONTINUED:

> PEARL
> Welcome "None of Your Business."
> Are we ready to play?

> OYSTERS
> Yes!

> PEARL
> Then let's spin the wheel.
> (OYSTERS cheer)
> Today's top prize is direction to
> the sea monster's lair.

> PEGGY
> That's what we need.

> SCUMMY
> But what if we lose? I've heard
> about the Wheel of Misfortune. All
> sorts of bad things happen to the
> losers.

> PEARL
> Let's tell you about the
> misfortunes on our wheel, shall we?

(OYSTERS cheer. Announcer is a voice over a microphone. An OYSTER in a blond wig can point at the follow items on the wheel)

> VOICE
> Thank you, Pearl. On the prize
> wheel, we have being stung by
> jellyfish...

> OYSTERS
> Oooh!

> VOICE
> Skewered by swordfish...

> OYSTERS
> Aaah!

> VOICE
> Tickled by tiger sharks...

> OYSTERS
> Oooh!

> VOICE
> Or gargled by a great white...

(CONTINUED)

CONTINUED: 20.

                    OYSTERS
          Aaah!

                    PEARL
          Thank you.
               (OYSTERS cheer)
          And thank you. (To PEGGY) Let's
          spin the wheel.

(PEARL or blond OYSTER spin wheel. OYSTERS cheer)

                    SCUMMY
          No, Peggy. We can't play. It's too
          dangerous.

                    PEGGY
          I don't think we have a choice.

                    SCUMMY
          We're doomed.

                    PEARL
          And the wheel stops on...

(Someone can be behind wheel controlling it or the wheel
prizes are turned away so audience can't see)

                    VOICE
          A brand new pearl!

(OYSTERS and SCUMMY cheer. One OYSTER comes over a coughs up
a pearl. OYSTERS cheer again as SCUMMY looks greedily)

                    PEARL
          Do you want this prize or do you
          want to spin again?

                    PEGGY
          We really need the directions to
          the sea monster's lair.

                    SCUMMY
          What?! Look at the size of that
          pearl. Are you crazy?

                    PEGGY
          Spin again.

                    SCUMMY
          No!

                                              (CONTINUED)

CONTINUED: 21.

> PEARL
> Spin the wheel!

> OYSTERS
> Oooh.

(Wheel stops on Sea Monster)

> VOICE
> Dinner with the Sea Monster!

(OYSTERS cheer)

> PEGGY
> We did it.

> SCUMMY
> I don't believe it.

> PEARL
> Personally, I would have taken the Pearl.

(PEARL hands PEGGY a map)

> PEGGY
> I have to rescue the other pirates.

> PEARL
> I still would have gone for the pearl.

(PEARL and OYSTERS exit with Wheel of Misfortune)

> SCUMMY
> Wait a minute... did you say dinner? Oh, dear.

> PEGGY
> On to the sea monster's lair!

(Lights fade to black)

SCENE 3

(Lights come up on an island where the sea monster lives. PEGGY and SCUMMY enter. SCUMMY is terrified)

> PEGGY
> This must be the sea monsters lair.

(CONTINUED)

CONTINUED: 22.

                    SCUMMY
          I don't think this is a good idea,
          Peggy.

                    PEGGY
          Yes, you said that about a hundred
          times on the way over. But someone
          has to save these pirates.

                    SCUMMY
          And what makes you think we can do
          it?

                    PEGGY
          Because I can do anything I put my
          mind to.

(Roaring sound off stage. SEA MONSTER uses microphone for big sound)

                    SCUMMY
          What's that?

                    PEGGY
          I don't know.

(Roaring sound again)

                    SCUMMY
          There is was again.
               (Roaring)
          Let's get out of here.

                    PEGGY
          But I don't see anything.

(A huge shadow appears behind them. Shadow is cast using a cut out behind a light or by the SEA MONSTER standing being a spotlight. SCUMMY sees it)

                    SCUMMY
          Ahh! Run!

(SCUMMY runs)

                    PEGGY
          Scummy! Get back here.
               (PEGGY stands ready and faces
               the shadow)
          I guess it's up to me. (Bravely
          calls out) Show yourself sea
          monster. I'm ready for you!

(CONTINUED)

CONTINUED: 23.

                    SEA MONSTER
                  (Roars. Off)
            You better run little pirate before
            I eat you.

                    PEGGY
            No, you better run before I eat
            you.

                    SEA MONSTER
                  (Off)
            What? You can't eat me.

                    PEGGY
            I can eat anything I want.

(SEA MONSTER enters. SEA MONSTER is not much bigger than
PEGGY. SEA MONSTER can be in a costume with one or two
actors inside. If two actors are in costume, one is the head
and the other works the hind end and tail)

                    SEA MONSTER
            Why aren't you scared?

                    PEGGY
            Hey! You're just a little guy.

                    SEA MONSTER
            Usually the shadow scares most of
            them away.

                    PEGGY
            How did you do that?

                    SEA MONSTER
            Ancient sea monster secret.

                    PEGGY
            Come on, you can tell me.

                    SEA MONSTER
            You're a pirate. I can't tell you.

                    PEGGY
                  (Proud)
            Hey, nobody has ever called me a
            pirate before.

                    SEA MONSTER
            That wasn't a compliment.

                                            (CONTINUED)

CONTINUED: 24.

                    PEGGY
          So what's the deal? How can a
          little monster like you defeat all
          those pirates?

                    SEA MONSTER
          Oh, that isn't me. That's my mama.
          She's the one who destroys all
          those ships.

                    PEGGY
          And she captured all those pirates?

                    SEA MONSTER
          Yes.

                    PEGGY
          Then I need to talk to her.

                    SEA MONSTER
          You can't do that.

                    PEGGY
          Why not?

                    SEA MONSTER
          She won't talk to you. She'll just
          capture you and torture you like
          the others.

                    PEGGY
          Torture?! That's terrible.

                    SEA MONSTER
          They are getting what they deserve.

                    PEGGY
          I won't hear of it. Take me to them
          or else.

                    SEA MONSTER
          Or else what?

                    PEGGY
          I... I....

                    SEA MONSTER
          You... you... what?

                    PEGGY
          I won't tell you my secret.

                                              (CONTINUED)

CONTINUED:

> SEA MONSTER
> Secret? What secret?

> PEGGY
> (To audience)
> Sea monsters can't resist a good secret. (To SEA MONSTER) I'll tell you if you take me to your mama.

> SEA MONSTER
> Give me a hint...

> PEGGY
> Nope. Not until I see you're mama.

> SEA MONSTER
> Not one little hint?

> PEGGY
> Sorry.

> SEA MONSTER
> Fine. I'll take you to Mama. She'll just capture though. She won't tell you anything. Follow me.

> SCUMMY
> (Sneaks up on them and stabs SEA MONSTER in the foot with a stick)
> Ha! I got you.

> SEA MONSTER
> Ow!

(SEA MONSTER hops around in pain)

> PEGGY
> Scummy! What have you done?

> SCUMMY
> I've defeated the sea monster!

> PEGGY
> But if you hurt the sea monster, we won't know where the pirates were taken.

> SCUMMY
> Oh.

(CONTINUED)

CONTINUED: 26.

                    SEA MONSTER
Who poked me? That hurts!

                    SCUMMY
         (Points to PEGGY)
She did it.

(SCUMMY runs)

                    SEA MONSTER
Come back here. I know a little
liar when I see one.

(SEA MONSTER takes a step and howls in pain)

                    PEGGY
Here, let me help you.

                    SEA MONSTER
Why would you want to do that?

                    PEGGY
Well... I do want you to show me
where the pirates are... but...

                    SEA MONSTER
But what?

                    PEGGY
I kind of like you too.

                    SEA MONSTER
You do?

                    PEGGY
I know pirates aren't supposed to
like sea monsters, but I do kind of
like you.

                    SEA MONSTER
And why is that?

                    PEGGY
Because you're little and you're so
big all at the same time. I wish I
could be as brave and strong as
you.

                    SEA MONSTER
I don't feel so brave and strong
with this stick in my foot.

(SEA MONSTER howls in pain)

                                        (CONTINUED)

CONTINUED: 27.

                    PEGGY
Here, let me help with that.

                    SEA MONSTER
              (Moves away)
No.

                    PEGGY
Come on.

                    SEA MONSTER
No, it's gonna hurt.

                    PEGGY
Don't be a baby. Let me get it.

                    SEA MONSTER
Fine, but I can't look.

                    PEGGY
On the count of three I'll pull it out. Ready?

                    SEA MONSTER
Ready.

                    PEGGY
One, two...

(PEGGY pulls out stick)

                    SEA MONSTER
...where's three?

(SEA MONSTER looks and PEGGY has stick)

                    PEGGY
Stick's out. See, it wasn't that bad was it.

                    SEA MONSTER
              (Looks at stick then howls)
Ow!

                    PEGGY
What? What?

                    SEA MONSTER
Now it hurts. Delayed reaction.

                    PEGGY
Don't be silly. It's all in your head.

(CONTINUED)

CONTINUED: 28.

>   SEA MONSTER
>   You think so?

>   PEGGY
>   I know so.

>   SEA MONSTER
>   I guess it's not that bad.

>   PEGGY
>   Good. Now take me to your mama.

>   SEA MONSTER
>   Uh, Peggy.

(A huge shadow looms up behind PEGGY. MAMA MONSTER can remain a shadow unless a production budget allows for a large monster head to appear on stage but this is unnecessary. A shadow cast by a cutout in a light will work with the voice of MAMA MONSTER on microphone)

>   PEGGY
>   Yes?

>   SEA MONSTER
>   She's here.

>   MAMA MONSTER
>   Hello, baby. Did you capture another pirate?

>   SEA MONSTER
>   Well, not really. This is Peggy. She wants to talk to you.

>   MAMA MONSTER
>   Talk to me? Why?

>   PEGGY
>   I want you to release all those pirates you captured.

>   MAMA MONSTER
>   Why?

>   PEGGY
>   Because what did they do to you?

>   MAMA MONSTER
>   They have made a garbage dump of the sea.

(CONTINUED)

CONTINUED:

PEGGY
You're mad at them because they litter.

SEA MONSTER
Pirates make a lot of trash.

PEGGY
But you're polluting the sea with broken pirate ships.

MAMA MONSTER
Good point. You're a smart little one.

PEGGY
I guess I make up for size with brains. That must be what that old coot meant. My brains! They must be bigger than any pirates.

SEA MONSTER
That's not saying much. I think my ear wax is smarter than most pirates.

PEGGY
So what did you do with the pirates?

MAMA MONSTER
We're making them pick up all the litter they've made.

SEA MONSTER
And that could take a long time. They've littered a lot.

PEGGY
Would you let them go if I could get them to stop littering?

SEA MONSTER
You really think you could get them to stop?

MAMA MONSTER
It won't be easy.

PEGGY
But if I could, would you let them go?

(CONTINUED)

CONTINUED: 30.

                    MAMA MONSTER
          Sure. Why not?

                    PEGGY
          Great. Point me to them. I'll talk
          to them right now.

                    SEA MONSTER
          They're resting over there. They
          have a five minute break every five
          hours.

                    MAMA MONSTER
          Good luck.

                    SEA MONSTER
          You'll need it.

                    PEGGY
          I'm sure once I explain the
          situation the pirates will be very
          reasonable.
                    (Laughs)
          Ha! That's a laugh. But I still
          have to try.

(PEGGY and SEA MONSTER exit. PIRATES enter and are sitting
around very tired)

                    BOB
          Can you believe how much trash is
          out there?

                    SUE
          Where did it all come from?

                    BOB
          That sea monster probably made it
          all.

                    SUE
          And now we have to clean up after
          it.

                    BOB
          Do I look like a garbage man?

                    SUE
          Well...

                    BOB
          You looking for a fight, mate?

                                                      (CONTINUED)

CONTINUED:

>   SUE
>   Relax. Save your energy for the
>   trash.
>
>   PEGGY
>   (Goes to them)
>   Hey, pirates!
>
>   BOB
>   Well, if it ain't Peggy the
>   pipsqueak.
>
>   SUE
>   You get captured too?
>
>   PEGGY
>   No, I'm here to rescue you.

(PIRATES laugh)

>   BOB
>   You? Rescue us?
>
>   PEGGY
>   It's true. I've got the Sea Monster
>   to agree to let you go.
>
>   SUE
>   And how did you do that? Did you
>   scare her with your huge size?
>
>   BOB
>   Did you arm wrestle her with your
>   big muscles?
>
>   SUE
>   Did you chase her around on your
>   long legs?

(PIRATES are all laughing)

>   PEGGY
>   No, I only had to talk to the Sea
>   Monster.
>
>   BOB
>   Talk to it?
>
>   SUE
>   Why would you talk to it?

(CONTINUED)

CONTINUED: 32.

                    PEGGY
          The sea monster is quite
          intelligent actually.

                    BOB
          A beast? Intelligent?

                    SUE
          No way is it as smart as any of us.

(PEGGY gives a look at the audience but resists saying anything)

                    PEGGY
          I got the sea monster to agree to
          let you go.

                    BOB
          No way.

                    SUE
          Really? Let's go then.

                    PEGGY
          But you have to stop littering.

                    BOB
          But we ain't littering.

(BOB throws down a wrapper in anger)

                    PEGGY
          Look. You just littered.

(BOB tosses another wrapper down angrily)

                    BOB
          I did not!

                    PEGGY
          You did it again.

                    BOB
          This is crazy.

(BOB tosses another wrapper and wanders off)

                    PEGGY
          Do you really want to be stuck here
          forever picking up trash?

                                              (CONTINUED)

CONTINUED: 33.

                    SUE
          Not really.

                    PEGGY
          Then make a promise and you can go.

                    SUE
          Just a promise, huh?

                    BOB
               (Comes back)
          That's it? One little promise.

                    PEGGY
          Yes.

                    BOB
          Sure, why not then.

(Winks at SUE)

                    SUE
          What do we do?

                    PEGGY
          Raise your right hands and say, "I
          promise not to litter."

                    BOB
          Okay, pirates. Swear.
               (PIRATES start saying things
               like "Aw, whale guts. Kill me
               a krill. Shoot me a shark.
               Scurvy dogs. Rats." And other
               silly swear words)
          No, no. The oath.

(They raise their rights hands and cross their fingers on
their left so PEGGY can't see)

                    PIRATES
          We promise not to litter.

                    PEGGY
          Good. I'll talk to the sea monster.

                    SUE
          Sure thing, Peggy. This way you
          scurvy dogs.

(PIRATES exit and SEA MONSTER appears along with giant
shadow of MAMA MONSTER)

                                                        (CONTINUED)

CONTINUED:

>PEGGY
>I promise that they will never litter again if you let them go.

>MAMA MONSTER
>Can I trust you? You're a pirate.

>SEA MONSTER
>She's not like other pirates, Mama. She helped me when I was hurt. She is also my friend.

>PEGGY
>Really?

>SEA MONSTER
>Really, really.

>MAMA MONSTER
>Pirates!
>>(PIRATES rush out and crowd together shaking in fear)
>
>I'll let them go, but I don't want to see any more litter. (PIRATES shake head no but have fingers crossed) Good-bye Peggy Pirate. I wish all pirates were like you.

(MAMA MONSTER exits/shadow fades)

>SEA MONSTER
>Good-bye, Peggy.

>PEGGY
>Will I see you again?

>SEA MONSTER
>You bet.
>>(SCUMMY slinks in cautiously. CAPTAIN SLUDGE and CAPTAIN SOGGY follow. CAPTAINS happily greet PIRATES)
>
>Just don't bring that thing with you.

(SEA MONSTER exits)

>SCUMMY
>>(Sees PIRATES)
>
>What happened?

(CONTINUED)

CONTINUED:

                    PEGGY
They set the pirates free.

                    SCUMMY
You saved them?

                    CAPTAIN SLUDGE
I never thought such a little pirate could do such a big thing.

                    CAPTAIN SOGGY
How would you like to be my first mate?

                    CAPTAIN SLUDGE
Three cheers for Peggy.

                    PIRATES
Hip-hip-hurray! Hip-hip-hurray! Hip-hip-hurray!

                    PEGGY
Thank you all of you. But this means no more litter.

(PIRATES nods in agreement)

                    CAPTAIN SLUDGE
Let's go, you scurvy dogs.

(PEGGY watches PIRATES go with CAPTAINS. CAPTAIN SOGGY tosses some litter in front of her. PEGGY's jaw drop when she sees the spot where they were standing. It's full of litter)

                    PEGGY
I see my work is cut out for me.

                    MAMA MONSTER
                    (Shadow appears)
Is that litter I see? (Big roar) Pirates!

(PIRATES yell and run across stage and off. Another big roar. Pirates run back across stage again)

                    PEGGY
Here we go again.

                    END OF PLAY

PEGGY THE PINT SIZED PIRATE (15 MINUTE FEMALE VERSION)

(7 characters plus optional extras)

Cast of Characters

PEGGY - a small pirate who sets out to rescue the pirates from a sea monster

SCUMMY - young pirate who says mean things to PEGGY

CAPTAIN SLUDGE - Pirate Captain who wants to plunder and pillage Arizona

CAPTAIN SOGGY - Pirate Captain who secretly wants to open a sea side resort

GRUNT - wise old pirate who speaks mysteriously

SEA MONSTER - a baby sea monster who helps his mama capture the pirates

MAMA MONSTER - a sea monster mother that is angry at the pirates for littering in her ocean

EXTRAS - Other PIRATES

Scene 1 - A pirate's cove for games and grub

Scene 2 - An island where the Sea Monster lurks
SCENE 1

(PEGGY is a very small pirate girl who is anxious to be a big pirate. PEGGY enters pirate's cove and sees Pirates playing various games and enjoying grub. Everyone is much bigger than she is and she looks out of place)

          PEGGY
     (To audience)
Hi, I'm Peggy. Peggy the... Well, I don't have a true pirate name yet.

          SCUMMY
     (To PEGGY)
Sure you do. It's Peggy the Pint Sized Pirate.

(Other pirates laugh and then go back to their games)

(CONTINUED)

CONTINUED:

                    PEGGY
          Yes, that's what they call me.
          Peggy the Pint Sized Pirate. But
          I'm tired of it. I won't stand for
          it anymore.

                    SCUMMY
          Won't stand for it? I thought you
          were sitting down.

                    PEGGY
          I'm so tired of short jokes.
          Anyway, Today is my big day. I
          finally was going to be a pirate.
          I've dreamed about this day since I
          was little.
               (SCUMMY looks at her)
          Well, I'm still little... and I'm
          still dreaming. But finally the day
          has come. I'm going to do it. I'm
          going to be a pirate.

(SCUMMY laughs at her and then points to CAPTAINS who enter)

                    SCUMMY
          Line em up!

(Pirates line up. PEGGY gets stuck behind the other pirates and hops around trying to see. She slips in between two of them)

                    CAPTAIN SOGGY
          We need two crews for a treasure
          run to Tucson.

                    PEGGY
          Tuscon?

(PEGGY gets pushed back and hops around behind)

                    CAPTAIN SLUDGE
          I get first pick. I'll take Bob the
          Brave

(BOB happily lines up behind SLUDGE)

                    CAPTAIN SOGGY
          I'll take Sue the Smelly.

(Everyone steps back so SUE can move over by SOGGY who

                                                (CONTINUED)

CONTINUED: 38.

notices her odor. SLUDGE and SOGGY continue picking pirates during the following:)

                    PEGGY
I was so excited. This was the first time I tried out for a pirate crew. Captain Sludge had the fastest pirate around. Everyone was anxious to be with Sludge when the sea speed record of 1812 was broken. And then Captain Soggy was great too. Soggy had the only pirate ship that would go underwater. Really! But after more and more pirates were picked, I got worried because no one was picking me.

                  CAPTAIN SLUDGE
And I'll take Scummy the Sweet.
     (SCUMMY sticks tongue out at
     PEGGY and lines up with
     others)
That's it then.

(Pirates all start to talk and go with CAPTAINS)

                    PEGGY
Wait! What about me?!

(Everyone stops and stares at PEGGY. Then they laugh)

                    SCUMMY
No way, shrimp.

                  CAPTAIN SOGGY
     (Pats PEGGY on head)

Maybe when you're bigger.

                    SCUMMY
Right, that will happen.

                  CAPTAIN SLUDGE
Better stay here and let the big brave pirates go. We don't want you to get hurt.

                  CAPTAIN SOGGY
We can't handle screaming little girls on ships with sea monster afoot.

(CONTINUED)

CONTINUED:

(Pirates leave and PEGGY sits by herself all upset)

              PEGGY
Now I'll never be a pirate.

(PEGGY cries. Old GRUNT enters)

              GRUNT
What's this boo-hooing I hear?

              PEGGY
No one wants me to be a pirate. They think I'm too little.

              GRUNT
Do they now?

              PEGGY
Everyone laughed at me and said I'd be scared. I'm not scared of anything. And I wouldn't cry...
    (Wipes away tears)
I'm not afraid of any sea monsters.
    (Cries again)
Who am I kidding? I am too little.

              GRUNT
You're not little at all you know.

              PEGGY
What? Can't you see me? I'm tiny.

              GRUNT
There's something I can see that's bigger than any pirate I know. Something that you'll have to see on your own.

              PEGGY
I don't get it. What do you mean?

              GRUNT
Give it time, Peggy and you'll see.

              PEGGY
    (Throwing a fit)
But I wanna be big now!!!!!!

(PEGGY jumps around and screams. GRUNT waits for PEGGY to stop)

(CONTINUED)

CONTINUED:

> GRUNT
> Feel better?

> PEGGY
> (Calm)
> Actually, yes. Thank you.

> GRUNT
> Very soon you'll get your chance to see what you have that is greater than most.

> PEGGY
> Well, I'm not moving from this spot until I find out.

> GRUNT
> Stubborn aren't we?

> PEGGY
> Peggy the Stubborn. Naw, doesn't sound right.

> GRUNT
> Patience Peggy. Your moment will come.

(GRUNT leaves)

> PEGGY
> Old people saw the weirdest things. Me being big? Now? But how? So I stayed here and waited for an answer. And it didn't take long.

> SCUMMY
> (Runs in)
> Ahh! The horror! The horror!

> PEGGY
> What is it, Scummy?

> SCUMMY
> Both ships are gone. Destroyed.

> PEGGY
> But how?

(CONTINUED)

CONTINUED: 41.

                    SCUMMY
          The sea monster!

                    PEGGY
          Really? And the pirates couldn't
          stop them.

                    SCUMMY
          They tried but the monster is too
          powerful. Both ships are gone
          forever.

                    PEGGY
          How did you survive?

                    SCUMMY
          I hid in a barrel when I saw the
          monster coming.

                    PEGGY
          You hid? That's not very piratey.

                    SCUMMY
          Please don't tell.

(SCUMMY runs and hides. CAPTAIN SLUDGE enters with CAPTAIN SOGGY)

                    CAPTAIN SLUDGE
          I can't believe our ships are gone.

                    CAPTAIN SOGGY
          And the entire crew was captured.

                    PEGGY
          What are you going to do?

                    CAPTAIN SLUDGE
          What can we do?

                    CAPTAIN SOGGY
          Maybe I'll open up a little sea
          side resort.

                    PEGGY
          You can't give up. What about your
          crew? You must save them.

(CONTINUED)

CONTINUED:

>   CAPTAIN SLUDGE
>   Sorry, but I'm not going out there
>   again. Not with that monster out
>   there.
>
>   CAPTAIN SOGGY
>   And I could serve soda pop and soup
>   with little tiny umbrellas in them.
>
>   PEGGY
>   So you're both a couple of
>   chickens.

(Both CAPTAINS stop and stare at her)

>   CAPTAIN SLUDGE
>   What did you say?
>
>   PEGGY
>   Chickens.
>   (Acts like a chicken)
>   Brock, brock, brock.
>
>   CAPTAIN SOGGY
>   I could put chicken between two
>   slices of bread. Someone showed me
>   that on the Sandwich Islands.

(CAPTAIN SOGGY exits)

>   CAPTAIN SLUDGE
>   Fine. You think you're so brave.
>   Then you be captain and take care
>   of that sea monster yourself.
>   (Sticks huge captain hat on
>   PEGGY and it covers her head)
>   Best of luck to you, Captain.
>   (Laughs and exits)
>
>   PEGGY
>   (Pulls off hat)
>   Captain? Was he serious? Even if he
>   wasn't, it doesn't matter. Someone
>   has to save those pirates.
>   (Grabs SCUMMY out of hiding)
>   Come on, Scummy. We're going to
>   save some pirates.

SCENE 2

(Lights come up on an island where the sea monster lives. PEGGY and SCUMMY enter. SCUMMY is terrified)

(CONTINUED)

CONTINUED: 43.

              PEGGY
I took a little boat with only Scummy to help row. We followed the trail of wrecked ships until we made our way to this little island that must be the sea monsters lair.

              SCUMMY
I don't think this is a good idea, Peggy.

              PEGGY
Yes, you said that about a hundred times on the way over. But someone has to save these pirates.

              SCUMMY
And what makes you think we can do it?

              PEGGY
Because I can do anything I put my mind to.

(Roaring sound off stage. SEA MONSTER can use a microphone in order to make it really loud and scary)

              SCUMMY
What's that?

              PEGGY
I don't know.

(Roaring sound again)

              SCUMMY
There is was again.
                (Hears roaring)
Let's get out of here.

              PEGGY
But I don't see anything.

(A huge shadow appears behind them. Shadow is cast using a cut out behind a light or by the SEA MONSTER standing being a spotlight. SCUMMY sees it)

              SCUMMY
Ahh! Run!

(SCUMMY runs)

(CONTINUED)

CONTINUED: 44.

				PEGGY
			Scummy! Get back here.
				(PEGGY stands ready and faces
				the shadow)
			I guess it's up to me.
				(Bravely calls out)
			Show yourself sea monster. I'm
			ready for you!

				SEA MONSTER
				(Roars. Off)
			You better run little pirate before
			I eat you.

				PEGGY
			No, you better run before I eat
			you.

				SEA MONSTER
				(Off)
			What? You can't eat me.

				PEGGY
			I can eat anything I want.

(SEA MONSTER enters and is not much bigger than PEGGY. SEA MONSTER can be in a costume with one or two actors inside. If two actors are in costume, one is the head and the other works the hind end and tail)

				SEA MONSTER
			Why aren't you scared?

				PEGGY
			Hey! You're just a little guy.

				SEA MONSTER
			Usually the shadow scares most of
			them away.

				PEGGY
			How did you do that?

				SEA MONSTER
			Ancient sea monster secret.

				PEGGY
			Come on, you can tell me.

				SEA MONSTER
			You're a pirate. I can't tell you.

							(CONTINUED)

                    PEGGY
               (Proud)
          Hey, no body has ever called me a
          pirate before.

                    SEA MONSTER
          That wasn't a compliment.

                    PEGGY
          So what's the deal? How can a
          little monster like you defeat all
          those pirates?

                    SEA MONSTER
          Oh, that isn't me. That's my mama.
          She's the one who destroys all
          those ships.

                    PEGGY
          And she captured all those pirates?

                    SEA MONSTER
          Yes.

                    PEGGY
          Then I need to talk to her.

                    SEA MONSTER
          You can't do that.

                    PEGGY
          Why not?

                    SEA MONSTER
          She won't talk to you. She'll just
          capture you and torture you like
          the others.

                    PEGGY
          Torture?! That's terrible.

                    SEA MONSTER
          They are getting what they deserve.

                    PEGGY
          I won't hear of it. Take me to them
          or else.

                    SEA MONSTER
          Or else what?

                                        (CONTINUED)

CONTINUED: 46.

                  PEGGY
I... I...

                SEA MONSTER
You... you... what?

                  PEGGY
I won't tell you my secret.

                SEA MONSTER
Secret? What secret?

                  PEGGY
   (To audience)
Sea monsters can't resist a good secret.
   (To SEA MONSTER)
I'll tell you if you take me to your mama.

                SEA MONSTER
Give me a hint!

                  PEGGY
Nope. Not until I see your mama.

                SEA MONSTER
Not one little hint?

                  PEGGY
Sorry.

                SEA MONSTER
Fine. I'll take you to Mama. She'll just capture though. She won't tell you anything. Follow me.

(SCUMMY sneaks up on them and stabs SEA MONSTER in the foot with a stick)

                  SCUMMY
Ha! I got you.

                SEA MONSTER
Ow!

(SEA MONSTER hops around in pain)

                  PEGGY
Scummy! What have you done?

(CONTINUED)

CONTINUED:

                    SCUMMY
          I've defeated the sea monster!

                    PEGGY
          But if you hurt the sea monster, we
          won't know where the pirates were
          taken.

                    SCUMMY
          Oh.

                    SEA MONSTER
          Who poked me? That hurts!

                    SCUMMY
               (Points to PEGGY)
          She did it.

(SCUMMY runs away)

                    SEA MONSTER
          Come back here. I know a little
          liar when I see one.

(SEA MONSTER takes a step and howls in pain)

                    PEGGY
          Here, let me help you.

                    SEA MONSTER
          Why would you want to do that?

                    PEGGY
          Well... I do want you to show me
          where the pirates are... but...

                    SEA MONSTER
          But what?

                    PEGGY
          I kind of like you too.

                    SEA MONSTER
          You do?

                    PEGGY
          I know pirates aren't supposed to
          like sea monsters, but I do kind of
          like you.

(CONTINUED)

CONTINUED: 48.

                SEA MONSTER
And why is that?

                PEGGY
Because you're little and you're so big all at the same time. I wish I could be as brave and strong as you.

                SEA MONSTER
I don't feel so brave and strong with this stick in my foot.

(SEA MONSTER howls in pain)

                PEGGY
Here, let me help with that.

                SEA MONSTER
    (Moves away)
No.

                PEGGY
Come on.

                SEA MONSTER
No, it's gonna hurt.

                PEGGY
Don't be a baby. Let me get it.

                SEA MONSTER
Fine, but I can't look.

                PEGGY
On the count of three I'll pull it out. Ready?

                SEA MONSTER
Ready.

                PEGGY
One, two...

(PEGGY pulls out stick)

                SEA MONSTER
...where's three?

                PEGGY
Stick's out. See, it wasn't that bad was it.

(CONTINUED)

CONTINUED: 49.

(SEA MONSTER looks and sees that PEGGY has the stick, then howls)

							SEA MONSTER
					Ow!

							PEGGY
					What? What?

							SEA MONSTER
					Now it hurts. Delayed reaction.

							PEGGY
					Don't be silly. It's all in your
					head.

							SEA MONSTER
					You think so?

							PEGGY
					I know so.

							SEA MONSTER
					I guess it's not that bad.

							PEGGY
					Good. Now take me to your mama.

							SEA MONSTER
					Uh, Peggy.

(A huge shadow looms up behind PEGGY. MAMA MONSTER can remain a shadow unless a production budget allows for a large monster head to appear on stage but this is unnecessary. A shadow cast by a cutout in a light will work with the voice of MAMA MONSTER on microphone)

							PEGGY
					Yes?

							SEA MONSTER
					She's here.

							MAMA MONSTER
					Hello, baby. Did you capture
					another pirate?

							SEA MONSTER
					Well, not really. This is Peggy.
					She wants to talk to you.

(CONTINUED)

MAMA MONSTER
Talk to me?

PEGGY
I want you to release all those pirates you captured.

MAMA MONSTER
Why?

PEGGY
Because they didn't do anything to you.

MAMA MONSTER
Yes, they did. They have made a garbage dump of the sea.

PEGGY
You're mad at them because they litter?

SEA MONSTER
Pirates make a lot of trash.

PEGGY
But you're polluting the sea with broken pirate ships.

MAMA MONSTER
Good point. You're a smart little one.

PEGGY
I guess I make up for size with brains. That must be what that old coot meant. My brains! They must be bigger than any pirates.

SEA MONSTER
That's not saying much. I think my ear wax is smarter than most pirates.

PEGGY
So what did you do with the pirates?

MAMA MONSTER
We're making them pick up all the messes they've made.

(CONTINUED)

CONTINUED: 51.

              SEA MONSTER
And that could take a long time.
They've littered a lot.

              PEGGY
I promise that they will never
litter again if you let them go.

              MAMA MONSTER
Can I trust you? You're a pirate.

              SEA MONSTER
She's not like other pirates, Mama.
She helped me when I was hurt. She
is also my friend.

              PEGGY
Really?

              SEA MONSTER
Really, really.

              MAMA MONSTER
Pirates!

(PIRATES rush out and crowd together shaking in fear)

              MAMA MONSTER (CONT.)
I'll let them go, but I don't want
to see any more litter.

(PIRATES shake head no with fingers crossed behind their backs)

              MAMA MONSTER (CONT.)
Good-bye Peggy Pirate. I wish all
pirates were like you.

(Shadows fades)

              SEA MONSTER
Good-bye, Peggy.

              PEGGY
Will I see you again?

              SEA MONSTER
You bet.

(SCUMMY slinks in cautiously. CAPTAIN SLUDGE and CAPTAIN SOGGY follow. CAPTAINS happily greet PIRATES)

              (CONTINUED)

CONTINUED:

>   SEA MONSTER (CONT.)
>   Just don't bring that thing with
>   you.

(SEA MONSTER exits)

>   SCUMMY
>   (Sees PIRATES)
>   What happened?

>   PEGGY
>   The sea monsters set the pirates
>   free.

>   SCUMMY
>   You saved them?

>   CAPTAIN SLUDGE
>   I never thought such a little
>   pirate could do such a big thing.

>   CAPTAIN SOGGY
>   How would you like to be my first
>   mate?

>   CAPTAIN SLUDGE
>   Three cheers for Peggy.

>   PIRATES
>   Hip-hip-hurray! Hip-hip-hurray!
>   Hip-hip-hurray!

>   PEGGY
>   Thank you all of you. But this
>   means no more litter.

(PIRATES nods in agreement)

>   CAPTAIN SLUDGE
>   Let's go, you scurvy dogs.

(PEGGY watches PIRATES go with CAPTAINS. CAPTAIN SOGGY tosses some litter in front of her. PEGGY's jaw drop when she sees the spot where they were standing. It's full of litter)

>   PEGGY
>   I see my work is cut out for me.

(CONTINUED)

CONTINUED: 53.

                        END OF PLAY

PETE THE PINT SIZED PIRATE (30 MINUTE MALE VERSION)

(14 characters plus optional extras)

By

D. M. Larson

CAST OF CHARACTERS

PETE - a small pirate who sets out to rescue the pirates from a sea monster

SCUMMY - young pirate who says mean things to PETE

BOB AND ROB THE BRAVE - Two brothers who pick on PETE.

SUE THE STRONG - Another mean pirate.

SAM THE SMELLY - A mad pirate

CAPTAIN SLUDGE - Pirate Captain who wants to plunder and pillage Arizona

CAPTAIN SOGGY - Pirate Captain who secretly wants to open a sea side resort

GRUNT - wise old pirate who speaks mysteriously

MERMAID (Oceanna) - helps PETE find the sea monster

WILLY (the whale) - someone who knows the way to the sea monster

BARNEY (the barnacle) - attached to the whale and mocks the whale constantly

PEARL (the oyster) - a game show host

VOICE (game show announcer) - she can be some kind of sea animal or mermaid

SEA MONSTER - a baby sea monster who helps his mama capture the pirates

MAMA MONSTER - a sea monster mother that is angry at the pirates for littering in her ocean

EXTRAS - more kids for pirates, sea animals, mermaids, etc.

SCENES

Scene 1 - A pirate's cove for games and grub

(CONTINUED)

CONTINUED:

Scene 2 - On the high seas

Scene 3 - An island where the Sea Monster lurks

SCENE 1

(PETE is a very small pirate boy who is anxious to be a big pirate. PETE enters Pirate's Cove and sees pirates playing various games and enjoying grub. Everyone is much bigger than she is and she looks out of place)

PETE

(To audience)

Hi, I'm Pete. Pete the... Well, I don't have a true pirate name yet.

SCUMMY

(To PETE)

Sure you do. It's Pete the Pint Sized Pirate.

(Others laugh and then go back to their games)

PETE

Yes, that's what they call me. Pete the Pint Sized Pirate. But I'm tired of it. I won't stand for it anymore.

SCUMMY

Won't stand for it? I thought you were sitting down.

PETE

I'm so tired of short jokes. Anyway... Today is my big day. I am finally going to be a pirate. I've dreamed about this day since I was little.

(SCUMMY looks at him)

Well, I'm still little... and I'm still dreaming. But finally the day has come. I'm going to do it. I'm going to be a pirate.

(BOB, ROB, SAM and SUE come and inspect PETE)

ROB

No way. Pirates have to be big.

(CONTINUED)

CONTINUED: 56.

> SUE
> And they have to be strong.

(SUE holds out her hand to arm-wrestle PETE)

> SCUMMY
> You scared that Sue will hurt you, Pete?

> PETE
> I know I'm not as strong as you / but I know I'll be a good pirate. I'm a hard worker.

> BOB
> Hard worker? Some of the best pirates are lazy.

> PETE
> And I'm sharp as a tack.

> SUE
> The only sharp thing a pirate needs is her sword.

(Pokes at PETE with her sword)

> PETE
> So if I'm not a big, dumb, lazy killer then I can't be a pirate?

> BOB

(Looks at SUE, then at PETE)
> Pretty much.

(SUE, SAM, ROB and BOB go back to what they were doing)

> PETE
> There must be someone who would like a hard working thinker like me.

(SCUMMY laughs at him and then points to CAPTAINS who enter)

> SCUMMY
> Line em up!

(Pirates line up. PETE gets stuck behind the other pirates and hops around trying to see. He slips in between two of them)

(CONTINUED)

CONTINUED: 57.

> CAPTAIN SOGGY
> We need two crews for a treasure run to Tucson.

> PETE
> Tucson?

(PETE gets pushed back and hops around behind)

> CAPTAIN SLUDGE
> I get first pick. I'll take Rob and Bob the Brave.

(BOB happily lines up behind SLUDGE)

> CAPTAIN SOGGY
> I'll take Sue the Strong and Sam the Smelly.

(Everyone steps back so SAM can move over by SOGGY who notices his odor. SLUDGE and SOGGY continue picking pirates during the following:)

[Monologue to the audience]

> PETE
> I was so excited. This was the first time I tried out for a pirate crew. Captain Sludge had the fastest pirate ship around. Everyone was anxious to be with Sludge when the sea speed record of 1812 was broken. And then Captain Soggy was great too. Soggy had the only pirate ship that would go underwater. Really! But after more and more pirates were picked, I got worried because no one was picking me.

> CAPTAIN SLUDGE
> And I'll take Scummy the Sweet.

(SCUMMY sticks tongue out at PETE and lines up with others)
> That's it then.

(Pirates all start to talk and go with CAPTAINS)

> PETE
> Wait! What about me?!

(Everyone stops and stares at PETE. Then they laugh)

(CONTINUED)

CONTINUED: 58.

>SCUMMY
No way, shrimp.

>CAPTAIN SOGGY

(Pats PETE on head)
>Maybe when you're bigger.

>SCUMMY
Right, like that will happen.

>CAPTAIN SLUDGE
Better stay here and let the big brave pirates go. We don't want you to get hurt.

>CAPTAIN SOGGY
We can't handle screaming little kids on ships with sea monster afoot.

(Pirates leave and PETE sits by himself all upset)

>PETE
Now I'll never be a pirate.

(PETE cries)

>GRUNT

(Old GRUNT enters)
>What's this boo-hooing I hear?

>PETE
No one wants me to be a pirate. They think I'm too little.

>GRUNT
Do they now?

>PETE
Everyone laughed at me and said I'd be scared. I'm not scared of anything. And I wouldn't cry...

(Wipes away tears)
>I'm not afraid of any sea monsters.

(Cries again)
>Who am I kidding? I am too little.

(CONTINUED)

CONTINUED:

                    GRUNT
          You're not little at all you know.

                    PETE
          What? Can't you see me? I'm tiny.

                    GRUNT
          There's something I can see that's
          bigger than any pirate I know.
          Something that you'll have to see
          on your own.

                    PETE
          I don't get it. What do you mean?

                    GRUNT
          Give it time, Pete and you'll see.

                    PETE
(Throwing a fit)
          But I wanna be big now!!!!!!

(Jumps around and screams)

                    GRUNT
(Waits for PETE to stop)
          Feel better?

                    PETE
(Calm)
          Actually, yes. Thank you.

                    GRUNT
          Very soon you'll get your chance to
          see what you have that is greater
          than most.

                    PETE
          Well, I'm not moving from this spot
          until I find out.

GRUNT

Stubborn aren't we?

                    PETE
          Pete the Stubborn. Naw, doesn't
          sound right.

(CONTINUED)

CONTINUED: 60.

                    GRUNT
          Patience Pete. Your moment will
          come.

(GRUNT leaves)

                    PETE
          Old people say the weirdest things.
          Me being big? Now? But how? Little
          did I know that out at sea,
          something was about to happen that
          would change my life forever.

(A make shift sea and pirate ship is pushed in at one side
of the stage by PIRATES and another make shift sea and ship
is pushed in on the opposite side. CAPTAIN SLUDGE, BOB, ROB
and other PIRATES are in one boat. CAPTAIN SOGGY, SAM and
SUE and other PIRATES are in the other)

                    CAPTAIN SOGGY
          Set sail for Tucson!

                    SUE
          Captain. I see something.

                    SEA MONSTER

(Pops up from sea and does a Jaws impression)
          Da-dum.

                    SUE
          Did you see it?

                    CAPTAIN SOGGY
          No.

                    SEA MONSTER
          Da-dum.

                    SAM
          There!

                    CAPTAIN SOGGY
          Whale ho!

                    SEA MONSTER
          Da-dum.

                    SUE
          That's no whale.

                                             (CONTINUED)

CONTINUED:

                    CAPTAIN SOGGY
          It's a...

                SUE, SAM AND SOGGY
SEA MONSTER!

                    SEA MONSTER
          Da-da, da-da, da-da.

(Attacks ship)

                    CAPTAIN SOGGY
          Everyone pirate for himself!

(Runs away screaming)

                        SUE
          Help! It's got me.

(SEA MONSTER drags off SUE and other PIRATES. Sinks ship)

                    CAPTAIN SLUDGE

(Sees with spy glass)
          Now wasn't that something.

                        BOB
          What'd you see?

                    CAPTAIN SLUDGE
          Looked like Captain Soggy's ship
          was sunk by a... sea monster.

                        ROB
          Sea monster? Are you mad?

                    SEA MONSTER

(Appears)
          Did somebody say Sea Monster?

                        BOB
          There it is!

(SEA MONSTER disappears)

                    CAPTAIN SLUDGE
          Where?

                        ROB
          It's gone.

(CONTINUED)

CONTINUED: 62.

                CAPTAIN SLUDGE
     Likely story. I think you're seeing
     things.

                SEA MONSTER

(Pops up so CAPTAIN can't see)
     Yoo-hoo.

                BOB
     There it is again!

                CAPTAIN SLUDGE

(Turns. SEA MONSTER disappears)
     Where?

                BOB
     Right there. I swear.

                CAPTAIN SLUDGE
     That's it. One more outburst out of
     you and you'll walk the plank.

                SEA MONSTER
     Yoo-hoo.

(Waves at BOB who points frantically but CAPTAIN SLUDGE is
turned away. SEA MONSTER grabs ROB, BOB and other PIRATES)

                BOB
     Mommy...

(CAPTAIN SLUDGE is left alone)

                CAPTAIN SLUDGE
     It's so quiet. It's like I'm
     totally alone...

(Looks)
     Where is everybody?

(Looks down)
     Why is my ship filling with water?

                SEA MONSTER

(Appears)
     I believe you're sinking.

                CAPTAIN SLUDGE
     You think so?

                                    (CONTINUED)

CONTINUED:

                    SEA MONSTER
Most definitely.

                    CAPTAIN SLUDGE
Can you be sure?

                    SEA MONSTER
Quite. Because I put the hole in it myself.

                    CAPTAIN SLUDGE
Oh dear. You're not...

                    SEA MONSTER
I am.

                    CAPTAIN SLUDGE
Oh dear. I better...

                    SEA MONSTER
Run!

(CAPTAIN SLUDGE screams and runs and SEA MONSTER sinks ship)

(Back to PETE at Pirate's Cove)

                    SCUMMY

(Runs in)

Ahh! The horror! The horror!

                    PETE
What is it, Scummy?

                    SCUMMY
Both ships are gone. Destroyed.

                    PETE
But how?

                    SCUMMY
The sea monster!

                    PETE
Really? And the pirates couldn't stop them.

                    SCUMMY
They tried but the monster is too powerful. Both ships are gone forever.

(CONTINUED)

CONTINUED:

                PETE
How did you survive?

              SCUMMY
I hid in a barrel when I saw the monster coming.

                PETE
You hid? That's not very piratey.

              SCUMMY
Please don't tell.

(SCUMMY runs and hides)

            CAPTAIN SLUDGE

(Enters with CAPTAIN SOGGY)
I can't believe our ships are gone.

            CAPTAIN SOGGY
And the entire crew was captured.

                PETE
What are you going to do?

            CAPTAIN SLUDGE
What can we do?

            CAPTAIN SOGGY
Maybe I'll open up a little sea side resort.

                PETE
You can't give up. What about your crew? You must save them.

            CAPTAIN SLUDGE
Sorry, but I'm not going out there again. Not with that monster out there.

            CAPTAIN SOGGY
And I could serve soda pop and soup with little tiny umbrellas in them.

                PETE
So you're both a couple of chickens.

(Both CAPTAINS stop and stare at her)

(CONTINUED)

CONTINUED: 65.

                    CAPTAIN SLUDGE
What did you say?

                          PETE
Chickens.

(Acts like a chicken)
Brock, brock, brock.

                    CAPTAIN SOGGY
I could put chicken between two slices of bread. Someone showed me that on the Sandwich Islands.

(CAPTAIN SOGGY exits)

                    CAPTAIN SLUDGE
Fine. You think you're so brave. Then you be captain and take care of that sea monster yourself.

(Sticks huge captain hat on PETE and it covers her head)
Best of luck to you, Captain.

(Laughs and exits)

                          PETE

(Pulls off hat)
Captain? Was he serious? Even if he wasn't, it doesn't matter. Someone has to save those pirates.

(Grabs SCUMMY out of hiding)
Come on, Scummy. We're going to save some pirates.

SCENE 2

(PETE and SCUMMY appear in a small boat [they can carry out a cutout of a boat that they carry on and stand behind].)

                          PETE
So I set sail trying to find our missing pirate friends. I knew that if I could save them, then I would prove that I was worthy of being a pirate.

                       SCUMMY
And I knew if I went along, the captains couldn't find me and string me up for running away.

(CONTINUED)

                    PETE
          But they ran away too. How can they
          get mad at you?

                    SCUMMY
          Good point. Let's go back and tell
          them that.

                    PETE
          No, we've already come this far.
          We're not going back.

                    SCUMMY
          But I'm...

                    PETE
          You're what?

                    SCUMMY
          I'm scared, okay? Happy now.

                    PETE
          It's okay to be scared.

                    SCUMMY
          No, it's not. Pirates don't get
          scared.

                    PETE
          I'll bet they do. They just don't
          tell anyone. But it's okay to get
          scared.

                    SCUMMY
          Are you scared?

                    PETE
          For some reason, no. I'm not sure
          why. You think I would be but I'm
          so set on finding those lost
          pirates that I haven't thought
          about being scared.

                    SCUMMY
          Wow, Pete. You're really something.

                    PETE
          Hey, did you just say something
          nice to me?

                    SCUMMY

(Embarrassed)
                    (MORE)

                                              (CONTINUED)

CONTINUED: 67.

                    SCUMMY (cont'd)
No.

                    PETE
Yes, you did.

                    SCUMMY
Can we stop talking now?

(Piles of broken ships are pushed in on opposite side of stage)

                    PETE
Look. Over there.

                    SCUMMY
What is it?

                    MERMAID
(Appears in front of them)
It's a pirate ship graveyard.

                    PETE
What a mess.

                    SCUMMY
Who are you?

                    MERMAID
I'm Oceanna.

                    PETE
A mermaid.

                    MERMAID
This is my home. But it's ruined.

                    PETE
What happened?

                    MERMAID
The pirates came here looking for treasure. The sea monster got mad and destroyed their ships.

                    PETE
The sea monster? Can you help me find it?

                    MERMAID
Why would you want to do that? Can't you see what happened to the last pirates who tried?

(CONTINUED)

CONTINUED:											68.

                    PETE
          I want to free the pirates that it
          captured.

                    MERMAID
          You are very brave little pirate.

                    SCUMMY
          No, he's just crazy.

                    MERMAID
          It's not safe. Please turn back
          before you meet the same fate as
          the others.

                    SCUMMY
          Good idea. Let's go home.

                    PETE
          I can't. I have sworn an oath to
          help them. Can't you show us the
          way?

                    MERMAID
          I don't know the way... but I think
          I know someone who does. I'll see
          if they'll talk to you.

                    PETE
          Thank you.

(MERMAID goes)

                    SCUMMY
          I can't believe you're asking for
          help.

                    PETE
          What's wrong with that?

                    SCUMMY
          Pirates don't ask for help. We do
          everything by instinct.

                    PETE
          No wonder you're always getting
          lost.

                    WILLY

(WILLY is a whale [played by a bigger actor] and has BARNEY
the barnacle [played by a smaller actor] attached to him)
          The mermaid said you were looking
          for some directions.

                                              (CONTINUED)

CONTINUED:

                    BARNEY
          Directions? You'd get lost in a
          bathtub.

                    WILLY
          Quiet you.

                    BARNEY
              (Mocking)
          Quiet you.

                    WILLY
          Will you get off of me?

                    BARNEY
          Will you get off of me?

                    SCUMMY
          What is wrong with you guys?

                    WILLY
          Barney here is a barnacle. Us
          whales get stuck with them
          sometimes.

                    SCUMMY
          Can't you get rid of him?

                    WILLY
          I've been trying.

                    BARNEY
          I've been trying... but you're
          stuck with me baby.

                    PETE
          Excuse me. I do hate to bother you,
          but do you know the way to the Sea
          Monster's lair?

                    WILLY AND BARNEY
          The Sea Monster!

                    WILLY
          You don't want to go there.

                    BARNEY
          The Sea Monster hates pirates.

                    SCUMMY
          So we should go home then.

(CONTINUED)

CONTINUED:

				PETE
			No, we're going.

				WILLY
			Looks like you have a barnacle too.

(WILLY and BARNEY laugh)

				SCUMMY
			I'm not a barnacle. He's the
			barnacle. I'm stuck with him.

				WILLY
			Why do you want to find the Sea
			Monster anyway?

				PETE
			We have to save the other pirates.

				WILLY
			But I don't like pirates. Why
			should I help you?

				BARNEY
			Cause I do.

(Points)
			It's that way.

				WILLY
			Don't tell them that.

				BARNEY
			Don't tell them that.

(WILLY starts to drag off BARNEY)

				PETE
			Thanks.

				BARNEY
			Any time.

(Dragged off by WILLY)

				SCUMMY
			Weirdos.

				PETE
			Let's go then.

(CONTINUED)

CONTINUED: 71.

                   SCUMMY
Do we have to? I got you this far. But this is where I turned back before and I plan to again.

                   PETE
Come on, Scummy. Don't you want to be a hero.

                   SCUMMY
A hero?

                   PETE
If you rescue the pirates, you'll probably get a whole treasure chest of gold...

                   SCUMMY
(Brightens)
Gold?

                   PETE
I bet they'll make you captain.

                   SCUMMY
(Excited)
Captain?
(Smiles)
Let's go!

                   PETE
Let's.

(PETE and SCUMMY make a motion like they are swimming and OYSTERS appear ahead of them. PEARL is the head OYSTER and is like a game show host. The other OYSTERS are like a studio audience. If extras are not available, someone could hold up signs to the audience and the audience could do the OYSTER lines. Or it could be Mermaids and other sea animals with OYSTERS)

                   PEARL
Thank you for tuning in to the...

             PEARL AND OYSTERS
WHEEL.... OF... MISFORTUNE!

(Wheel is rolled out)

(CONTINUED)

CONTINUED:

>   PEARL
>   I'm your host Pearl Jam.

(OYSTERS cheer)
>   And I see we have a couple of new
>   contestants.

(Goes to PETE and SCUMMY)
>   Please tell us your names and a
>   little bit about yourselves.

>   PETE
>   Hi, I'm Pete.

>   OYSTERS
>   Hi, Pete.

>   PETE
>   And I'm looking for some pirates
>   who were kidnapped by a sea
>   monster.

(OYSTERS go "aaah!")
>   PEARL
>   How exciting!

(To SCUMMY)
>   And you are?

>   SCUMMY
>   None of your business.

(OYSTERS go "oooh!")
>   PEARL
>   Welcome None of Your Business. Are
>   we ready to play?

>   OYSTERS
>   Yes!

>   PEARL
>   Then let's spin the wheel.

(OYSTERS cheer)
>   Today's top prize... directions to
>   the sea monster's lair.

>   PETE
>   That's what we need.

(CONTINUED)

CONTINUED:

>   SCUMMY
>   But what if we lose? I've heard
>   about the Wheel of Misfortune. All
>   sorts of bad things happen to the
>   losers.
>
>   PEARL
>   Let's tell you about the
>   misfortunes on our wheel, shall we?

(OYSTERS cheer)

>   VOICE

(Announcer voice over microphone. An OYSTER in a blond wig can point at the follow items on the wheel)
>   Thank you, Pearl. On the prize
>   wheel, we have being stung by
>   jellyfish...

(OYSTERS go "oooh!")
>   Skewered by swordfish...

(OYSTERS go "aaah!")
>   Tickled by tiger sharks...

(OYSTERS go "oooh!")
>   Or gargled by a great white...

(OYSTERS go "aaah!")

>   PEARL
>   Thank you.

(OYSTERS cheer)
>   And thank you.

(To PETE)
>   Let's spin the wheel.

(PEARL or blond OYSTER spin wheel. OYSTERS cheer)

>   SCUMMY
>   No, Pete. We can't play. It's too
>   dangerous.
>
>   PETE
>   I don't think we have a choice.
>
>   SCUMMY
>   We're doomed.

(CONTINUED)

CONTINUED: 74.

>   PEARL
>   And the wheel stops on...

(Someone can be behind wheel controlling it or the wheel prizes are turned away so audience can't see)

>   VOICE
>   A brand new pearl!

(OYSTERS and SCUMMY cheer. One OYSTER comes over a coughs up a pearl. OYSTERS cheer again as SCUMMY looks greedily)

>   PEARL
>   Do you want this prize or do you
>   want to spin again?

>   PETE
>   We really need the directions to
>   the sea monster's lair.

>   SCUMMY
>   What?! Look at the size of that
>   pearl. Are you crazy?

>   PETE
>   Spin again.

>   SCUMMY
>   No!

>   PEARL
>   Spin the wheel!

(OYSTERS say "oooh." Wheel stops on Sea Monster)

>   VOICE
>   Dinner with the Sea Monster!

(OYSTERS cheer)

>   PETE
>   We did it.

>   SCUMMY
>   I don't believe it.

>   PEARL
>   Personally, I would have taken the
>   Pearl.

(Hands PETE a map)

(CONTINUED)

CONTINUED:

> PETE
> I have to rescue the other pirates.

> PEARL
> I still would have gone for the pearl.

(OYSTERS exit)

> SCUMMY
> Wait a minute... did you say dinner? Oh, dear.

> PETE
> On to the sea monster's lair!

(Lights fade to black)

SCENE 3

(Lights come up on an island where the sea monster lives. PETE and SCUMMY enter. SCUMMY is terrified)

> PETE
> This must be the sea monsters lair.

> SCUMMY
> I don't think this is a good idea, Pete.

> PETE
> Yes, you said that about a hundred times on the way over. But someone has to save these pirates.

> SCUMMY
> And what makes you think we can do it?

> PETE
> Because I can do anything I put my mind to.

(Roaring sound off stage. SEA MONSTER uses microphone for big sound)

> SCUMMY
> What's that?

> PETE
> I don't know.

(Roaring sound again)

(CONTINUED)

CONTINUED: 76.

                         SCUMMY
               There it is again.

(Roaring)
               Let's get out of here.

                         PETE
               But I don't see anything.

                         SCUMMY

(A huge shadow appears behind them. Shadow is cast using a
cut out behind a light or by the SEA MONSTER standing being
a spotlight. SCUMMY sees it)
               Ahh! Run!

(SCUMMY runs)

                         PETE
               Scummy! Get back here.

(PETE stands ready and faces the shadow)
               I guess it's up to me.

(Bravely calls out)
               Show yourself sea monster. I'm
               ready for you!

                         SEA MONSTER

(Roars. Off)
               You better run little pirate before
               I eat you.

                         PETE
               No, you better run before I eat
               you.

                         SEA MONSTER

(Off)
               What? You can't eat me.

                         PETE
               I can eat anything I want.

                         SEA MONSTER

(Enters. SEA MONSTER is not much bigger than PETE. SEA
MONSTER can be in a costume with one or two actors inside.
If two actors are in costume, one is the head and the other
works the hind end and tail)
               Why aren't you scared?

                                                    (CONTINUED)

CONTINUED: 77.

              PETE
     Hey! You're just a little guy.

              SEA MONSTER
     Usually the shadow scares most of
     them away.

              PETE
     How did you do that?

              SEA MONSTER
     Ancient sea monster secret.

              PETE
     Come on, you can tell me.

              SEA MONSTER
     You're a pirate. I can't tell you.

              PETE
(Proud)
     Hey, no body has ever called me a
     pirate before.

              SEA MONSTER
     That wasn't a compliment.

              PETE
     So what's the deal? How can a
     little monster like you defeat all
     those pirates?

              SEA MONSTER
     Oh, that isn't me. That's my mama.
     She's the one who destroys all
     those ships.

              PETE
     And she captured all those pirates?

              SEA MONSTER
     Yes.

              PETE
     Then I need to talk to her.

              SEA MONSTER
     You can't do that.

              PETE
     Why not?

(CONTINUED)

CONTINUED: 78.

>   SEA MONSTER
>   She won't talk to you. She'll just
>   capture you and torture you like
>   the others.
>
>   PETE
>   Torture?! That's terrible.
>
>   SEA MONSTER
>   They are getting what they deserve.
>
>   PETE
>   I won't hear of it. Take me to them
>   or else.
>
>   SEA MONSTER
>   Or else what?
>
>   PETE
>   I... I...
>
>   SEA MONSTER
>   You... you... what?
>
>   PETE
>   I won't tell you my secret.
>
>   SEA MONSTER
>   Secret? What secret?
>
>   PETE

(To audience)
>   Sea monsters can't resist a good
>   secret.

(To SEA MONSTER)
>   I'll tell you if you take me to
>   your mama.
>
>   SEA MONSTER
>   Give me a hint...
>
>   PETE
>   Nope. Not until I see you're mama.
>
>   SEA MONSTER
>   Not one little hint?
>
>   PETE
>   Sorry.

(CONTINUED)

CONTINUED: 79.

SEA MONSTER
Fine. I'll take you to Mama. She'll just capture you though. She won't tell you anything. Follow me.

SCUMMY

(Sneaks up on them and stabs SEA MONSTER in the foot with a stick)
Ha! I got you.

SEA MONSTER
Ow!

(Hops around in pain)

PETE
Scummy! What have you done?

SCUMMY
I've defeated the sea monster!

PETE
But if you hurt the sea monster, we won't know where the pirates were taken.

SCUMMY
Oh.

SEA MONSTER
Who poked me? That hurts!

SCUMMY

(Points to PETE)
He did it.

(SCUMMY runs)

SEA MONSTER
Come back here. I know a little liar when I see one.

(Takes a step and howls in pain)

PETE
Here, let me help you.

SEA MONSTER
Why would you want to do that?

(CONTINUED)

CONTINUED: 80.

                    PETE
          Well... I do want you to show me
          where the pirates are... but...

                    SEA MONSTER
          But what?

                    PETE
          I kind of like you too.

                    SEA MONSTER
          You do?

                    PETE
          I know pirates aren't supposed to
          like sea monsters, but I do kind of
          like you.

                    SEA MONSTER
          And why is that?

                    PETE
          Because you're little and you're so
          big all at the same time. I wish I
          could be as brave and strong as
          you.

                    SEA MONSTER
          I don't feel so brave and strong
          with this stick in my foot.

(Howls in pain)

                    PETE
          Here, let me help with that.

                    SEA MONSTER

(Moves away)
          No.

                    PETE
          Come on.

                    SEA MONSTER
          No, it's gonna hurt.

                    PETE
          Don't be a baby. Let me get it.

                    SEA MONSTER
          Fine, but I can't look.

                                        (CONTINUED)

CONTINUED: 81.

                         PETE
               On the count of three I'll pull it
               out. Ready?

                         SEA MONSTER
               Ready.

                         PETE
               One, two...

(Pulls out stick)

                         SEA MONSTER
               ...where's three.

(Looks)

                         PETE
               Stick's out. See, it wasn't that
               bad was it.

                         SEA MONSTER

(Looks at stick then howls)
               Ow!

                         PETE
               What? What?

                         SEA MONSTER
               Now it hurts. Delayed reaction.

                         PETE
               Don't be silly. It's all in your
               head.

                         SEA MONSTER
               You think so?

                         PETE
               I know so.

                         SEA MONSTER
               I guess it's not that bad.

                         PETE
               Good. Now take me to your mama.

                         SEA MONSTER
               Uh, Pete.

                                              (CONTINUED)

CONTINUED: 82.

(Huge shadow looms up behind PETE. MAMA MONSTER can remain a shadow unless a production budget allows for a large monster head to appear on stage but this is unnecessary. A shadow cast by a cutout in a light will work with the voice of MAMA MONSTER on microphone)

PETE
Yes?

SEA MONSTER
She's here.

MAMA MONSTER
Hello, baby. Did you capture another pirate?

SEA MONSTER
Well, not really. This is Pete. He wants to talk to you.

MAMA MONSTER
Talk to me? Why?

PETE
I want you to release all those pirates you captured.

MAMA MONSTER
Why?

PETE
Because what did they do to you?

MAMA MONSTER
They have made a garbage dump of the sea.

PETE
You're mad at them because they litter.

SEA MONSTER
Pirates make a lot of trash.

PETE
But you're polluting the sea with broken pirate ships.

MAMA MONSTER
Good point. You're a smart little one.

(CONTINUED)

CONTINUED: 83.

                         PETE
               I guess I make up for size with
               brains. That must be what that old
               coot meant. My brains! They must be
               bigger than any pirates.

                         SEA MONSTER
               That's not saying much. I think my
               ear wax is smarter than most
               pirates.

                         PETE
               So what did you do with the
               pirates?

                         MAMA MONSTER
               We're making them pick up all the
               litter they've made.

                         SEA MONSTER
               And that could take a long time.
               They've littered a lot.

                         PETE
               Would you let them go if I could
               get them to stop littering?

                         SEA MONSTER
               You really think you could get them
               to stop?

                         MAMA MONSTER
               It won't be easy.

                         PETE
               But if I could, would you let them
               go?

                         MAMA MONSTER
               Sure. Why not?

                         PETE
               Great. Point me to them. I'll talk
               to them right now.

                         SEA MONSTER
               They're resting over there. They
               have a five minute break every five
               hours.

                         MAMA MONSTER
               Good luck.

                                                          (CONTINUED)

CONTINUED:

                    SEA MONSTER
          You'll need it.

                    PETE
          I'm sure once I explain the
          situation the pirates will be very
          reasonable.

(Laughs)
          Ha! That's a laugh. But I still
          have to try.

(PETE and SEA MONSTER exit)

(PIRATES enter and are sitting around very tired)

                    ROB
          Can you believe how much trash is
          out there?

                    SUE
          Where did it all come from?

                    BOB
          That sea monster probably made it
          all.

                    SUE
          And now we have to clean up after
          it.

                    ROB
          Do I look like a garbage man?

                    SUE
          Well...

                    BOB
          You looking for a fight, mate?

                    SUE
          Relax. Save your energy for the
          trash.

                    PETE
(Goes to them)
          Hey, pirates!

                    ROB
          Well, if it ain't Pete the
          pipsqueak.

(CONTINUED)

CONTINUED: 85.

                    SUE
          You get captured too?

                    PETE
          No, I'm here to rescue you.

(PIRATES laugh)

                    BOB
          You? Rescue us?

                    PETE
          It's true. I've got the Sea Monster
          to agree to let you go.

                    SUE
          And how did you do that? Did you
          scare her with your huge size?

                    ROB
          Did you arm wrestle her with your
          big muscles?

                    SUE
          Did you chase her around on your
          long legs?

(PIRATES are all laughing)

                    PETE
          No, I only had to talk to the Sea
          Monster.

                    BOB
          Talk to it?

                    SUE
          Why would you talk to it?

                    PETE
          The sea monster is quite
          intelligent actually.

                    ROB
          A beast? Intelligent?

                    SUE
          No way is it as smart as any of us.

(PETE gives a look at the audience but resists saying anything)

(CONTINUED)

CONTINUED: 86.

              PETE
I got the sea monster to agree to let you go.

              ROB
No way.

              SUE
Really? Let's go then.

              PETE
But you have to stop littering.

              BOB
But we ain't littering.

(Throws down a wrapper in anger)

              PETE
Look. You just littered.

              BOB

(Tosses another wrapper down angrily)
I did not!

              PETE
You did it again.

              BOB
This is crazy.

(Tosses another wrapper and wanders off)

              PETE
Do you really want to be stuck here forever picking up trash?

              SUE
Not really.

              PETE
Then make a promise and you can go.

              SUE
Just a promise, huh?

              ROB
That's it? One little promise.

              PETE
Yes.

(CONTINUED)

CONTINUED: 87.

>   ROB
>   Sure, why not then.

(Winks at SUE)

>   SUE
>   What do we do?
>
>   PETE
>   Raise your right hands and say, "I
>   promise not to litter."
>
>   ROB
>   Okay, pirates. Swear.

(PIRATES start saying things like "Aw, whale guts. Kill me a krill. Shoot me a shark. Scurvy dogs. Rats." And other silly swear words)

>   No, no. The oath.

(They raise their rights hands and cross their fingers on their left so PETE can't see)

>   PIRATES
>   We promise not to litter.
>
>   PETE
>   Good. I'll talk to the sea monster.
>
>   SUE
>   Sure thing, Pete. This way you
>   scurvy dogs.

(PIRATES exit and SEA MONSTER appears along with giant shadow of MAMA MONSTER)

>   PETE
>   I promise that they will never
>   litter again if you let them go.
>
>   MAMA MONSTER
>   Can I trust you? You're a pirate.
>
>   SEA MONSTER
>   He's not like other pirates, Mama.
>   He helped me when I was hurt. He is
>   also my friend.
>
>   PETE
>   Really?

(CONTINUED)

CONTINUED: 88.

                    SEA MONSTER
        Really, really.

                    MAMA MONSTER
        Pirates!

(PIRATES rush out and crowd together shaking in fear)
        I'll let them go, but I don't want
        to see any more litter.

(PIRATES shake head no but have fingers crossed)
        Good-bye Pete Pirate. I wish all
        pirates were like you.

(Shadows fades)

                    SEA MONSTER
        Good-bye, Pete.

                    PETE
        Will I see you again?

                    SEA MONSTER
        You bet.

(SCUMMY slinks in cautiously. CAPTAIN SLUDGE and CAPTAIN SOGGY follow. CAPTAINS happily greet PIRATES)
        Just don't bring that thing with
        you.

(SEA MONSTER exits)

                    SCUMMY

(Sees PIRATES)
        What happened?

                    PETE
        They set the pirates free.

                    SCUMMY
        You saved them.

                    CAPTAIN SLUDGE
        I never thought such a little
        pirate could do such a big thing.

                    CAPTAIN SOGGY
        How would you like to be my first
        mate?

(CONTINUED)

CONTINUED:

                    CAPTAIN SLUDGE
         Three cheers for Pete.

                    PIRATES
         Hip-hip-hurray! Hip-hip-hurray!
         Hip-hip-hurray!

                    PETE
         Thank you all of you. But this
         means no more litter.

(PIRATES nods in agreement)

                    CAPTAIN SLUDGE
         Let's go, you scurvy dogs.

(PETE watches PIRATES go with CAPTAINS. CAPTAIN SOGGY tosses some litter in front of her. PETE's jaw drop when she sees the spot where they were standing. It's full of litter)

                    PETE
         I see my work is cut out for me.

                    MAMA MONSTER

(Shadow appears)
         Is that litter I see?

(Big roar)
         Pirates!

(PIRATES yell and run across stage and off. Another big roar. Pirates run back across stage again)

                    PETE
         Here we go again.

                    END OF PLAY

ADAPTED MONOLOGUE #1

"Little Pirate" Monologue for Female

PEGGY

(To audience)

Hi, I'm Peggy. Peggy the... Well, I don't have a true pirate name yet.

Well, some of them call me... Peggy the Pint Sized Pirate. But I'm tired of it. I won't stand for it anymore.

(Hears someone and put hands on hips)
Yes, I'm standing.

I'm so tired of short jokes. Anyway, Today is my big day. I finally am going to be a pirate. I've dreamed about this day since I was little.

Well, I'm still little... and I'm still dreaming. But finally the day has come. I'm going to do it. I'm going to be a pirate.

I am so excited. This is the first time I have tried out for a pirate crew. But after more and more pirates were picked, I got worried because no one was picking me. And then they stopped picking and walked away. They didn't even see me!

Wait! What about me?!

Now I'll never be a pirate.

(PEGGY cries)

END

ADAPTED MONOLOGUE #2

"Little Pirate" Monologue for Male

           PETE
     (To audience)

    Hi, I'm Pete. Pete the... Well, I don't have a true pirate name yet. Well, some of them call me... Pete the Pint Sized Pirate. But I'm tired of it. I won't stand for it anymore.

(Shakes his fist at someone in the audience)
    Yes, I'm standing.
    I'm so tired of short jokes.
    Anyway, Today is my big day. I finally am going to be a pirate. I've dreamed about this day since I was little.
    Well, I'm still little... and I'm still dreaming. But finally the day has come. I'm going to do it. I'm going to be a pirate.
    I am so excited. This is the first time I have tried out for a pirate crew. But after more and more pirates were picked, I got worried because no one was picking me. And then they stopped picking and walked away. They didn't even see me!
    Wait! What about me?!
    Now I'll never be a pirate.

(Pete fights back the tears and walks off sadly)

           END

Printed in Poland
by Amazon Fulfillment
Poland Sp. z o.o., Wrocław